How to Create Quilted Christmas Cards

A Guide to Designing and Making Beautiful Quilted Christmas Cards

By Debby Masten Berard

North Carolina Quilt Artist

For Andy, Lauren, and Matthew

This is NOT your mother's quilting!!

Table of Contents

1. Supplies
2. Sewing
3. Thoughts on Design
4. The Process
5. Christmas Card Ideas
6. Afterword
7. Acknowledgements
8. About the Author

Part I-Supplies

1. Fabric-I prefer upholstery fabric for the rich color and texture.
2. Cutting matt
3. Rotary cutter
4. Ruler
5. Fabric bonding

6. Iron
7. Sewing machine-free motion presser foot
8. Stickers
9. Beads
10. Blank 4" x 6" greeting cards-available at craft stores

Part II - Sewing

1. Cut a rectangle of fabric 5" x 3.5"
2. Cut accent fabrics- circles, straight lines or random shapes.
3. Press fabric bonding to back of accent fabric.
4. Press accent fabric to rectangle.
5. Use the free motion presser foot and stitch your rectangle to one end of the flat card.
6. Embellish with stickers.
7. Add beads.
8. Sign your name to back of card.

Part III - Thoughts on Design

1. Your cards will improve with experience.

2. Golden Rule of Design-Less is more.

3. Odd numbers look best.

4. Asymmetrical works well.

5. Combine stickers from different sheets.

6. Overlap stickers for better visual effect.

The Process

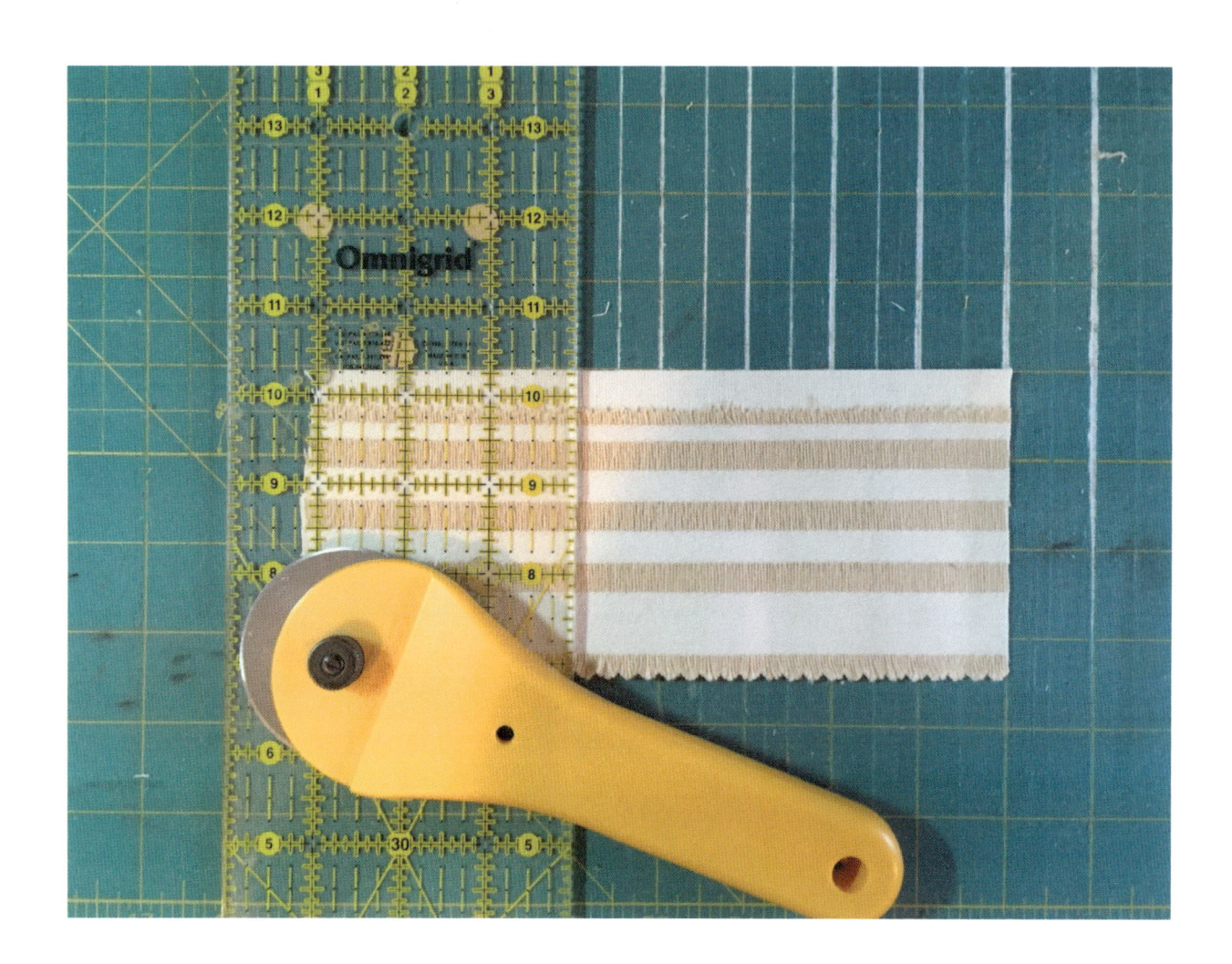

Cut the rectangle
using your matt and rotary
cutter.

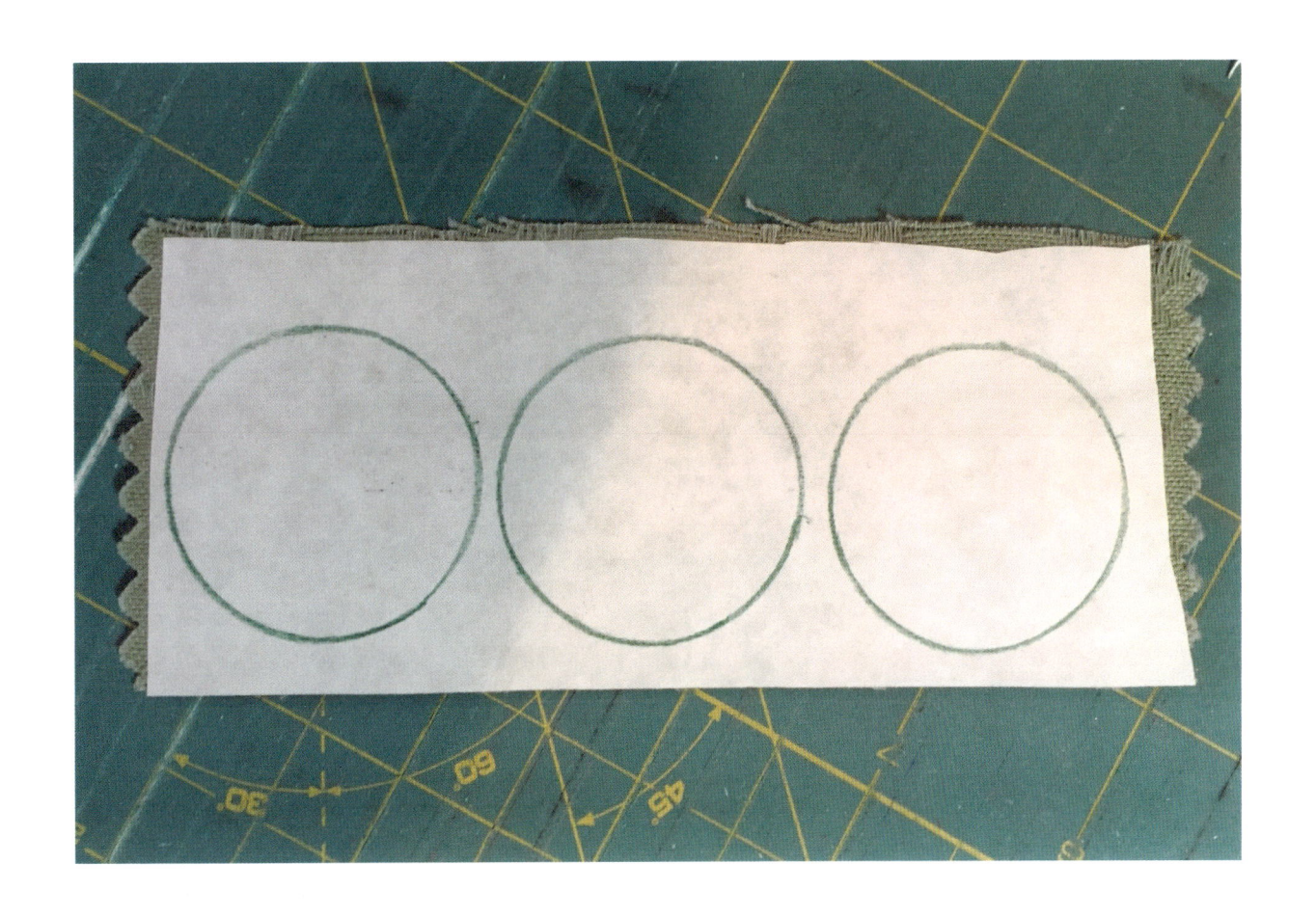

Press fabric bonding to back of accent fabric.

Press the circles to rectangle with bonding Facing down.

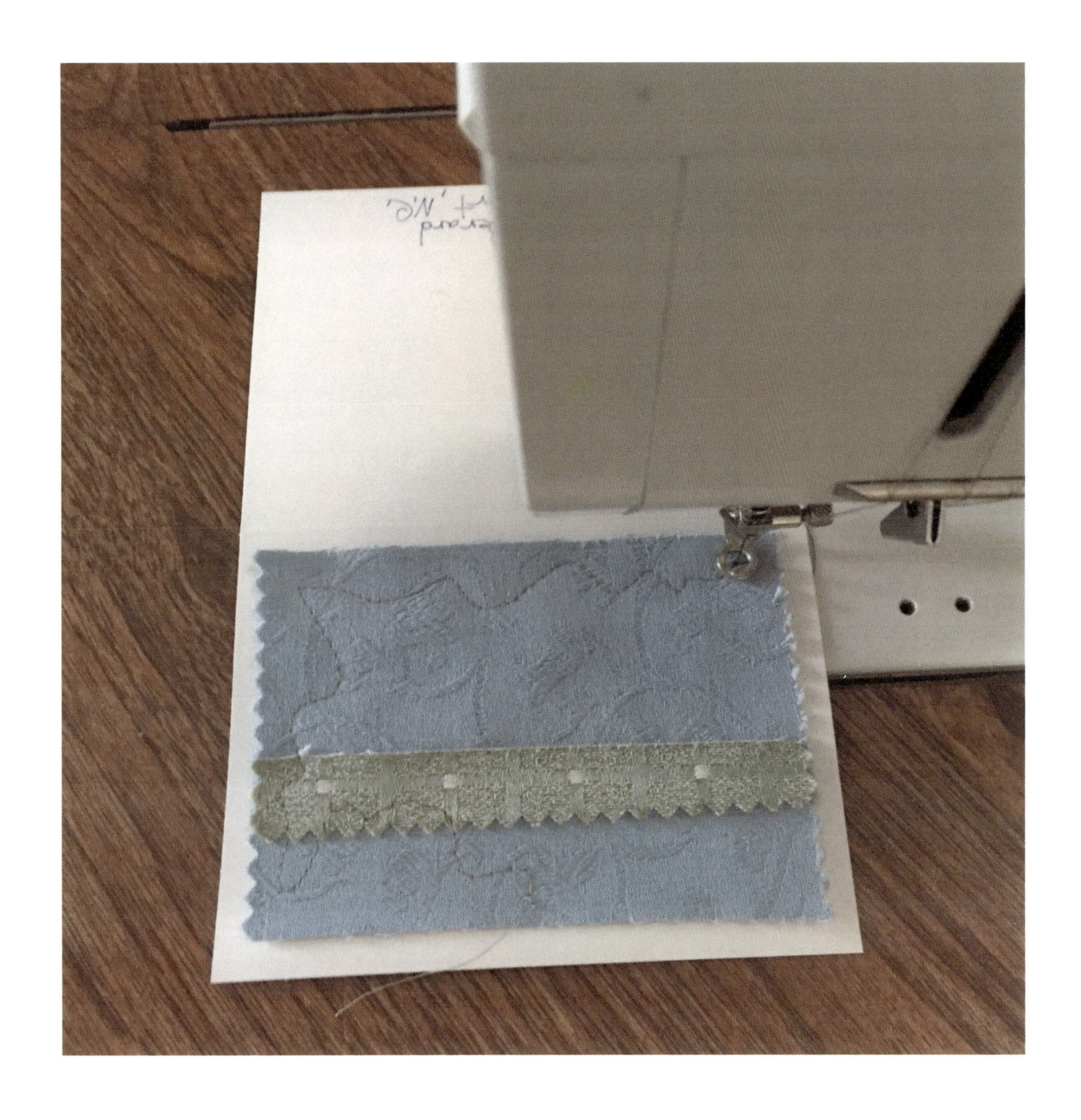

Use free motion presser foot and stitch through half of open card.

Christmas Card Ideas

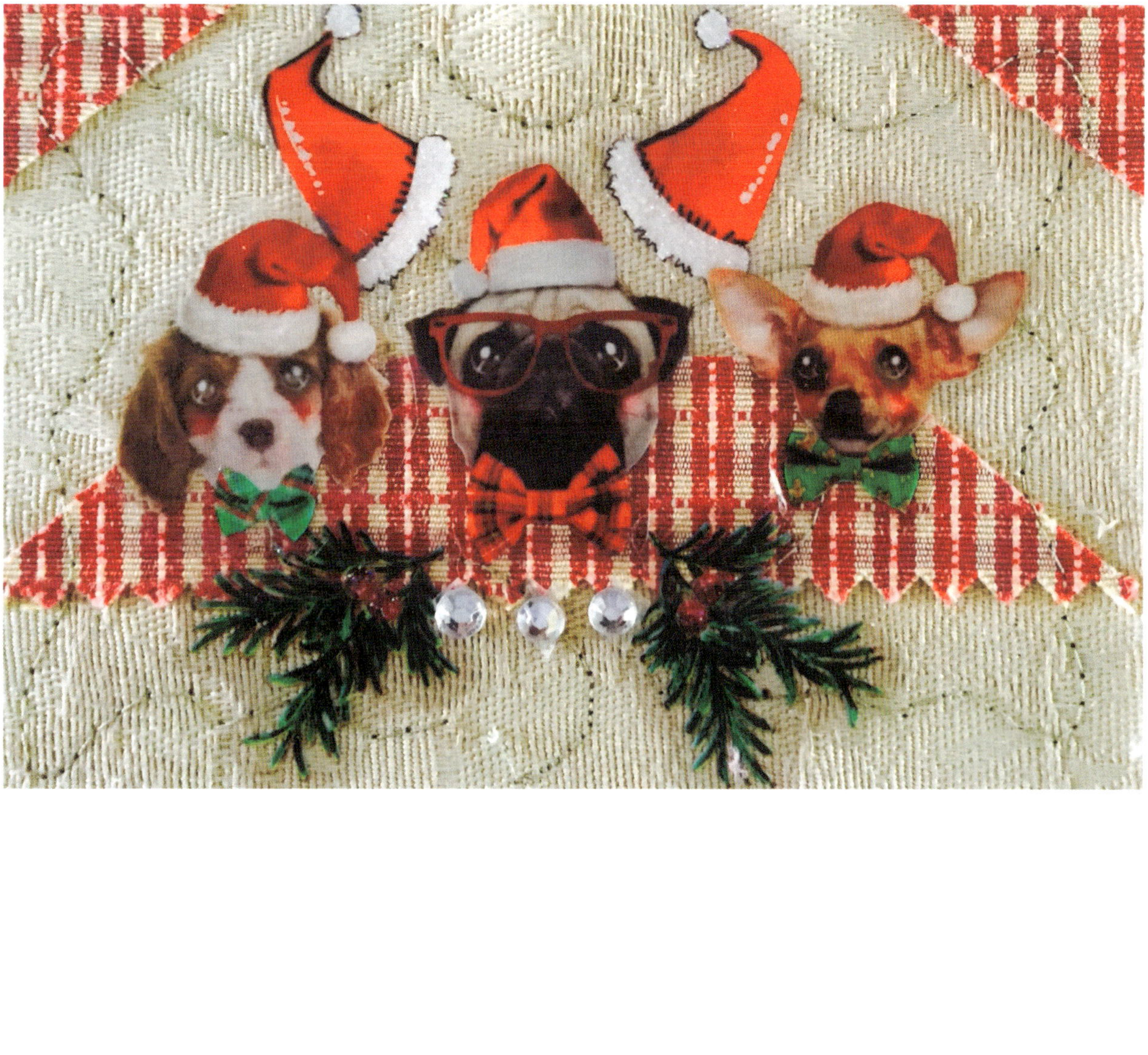

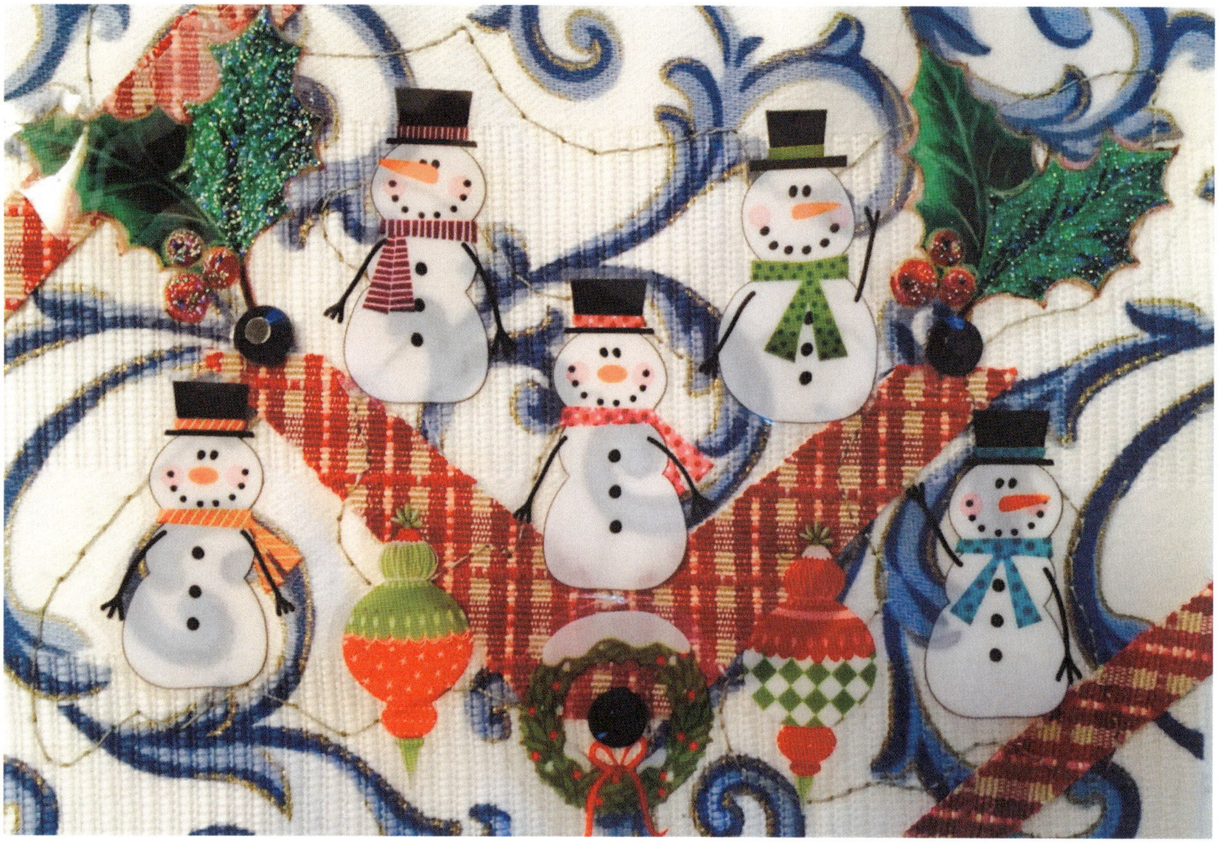

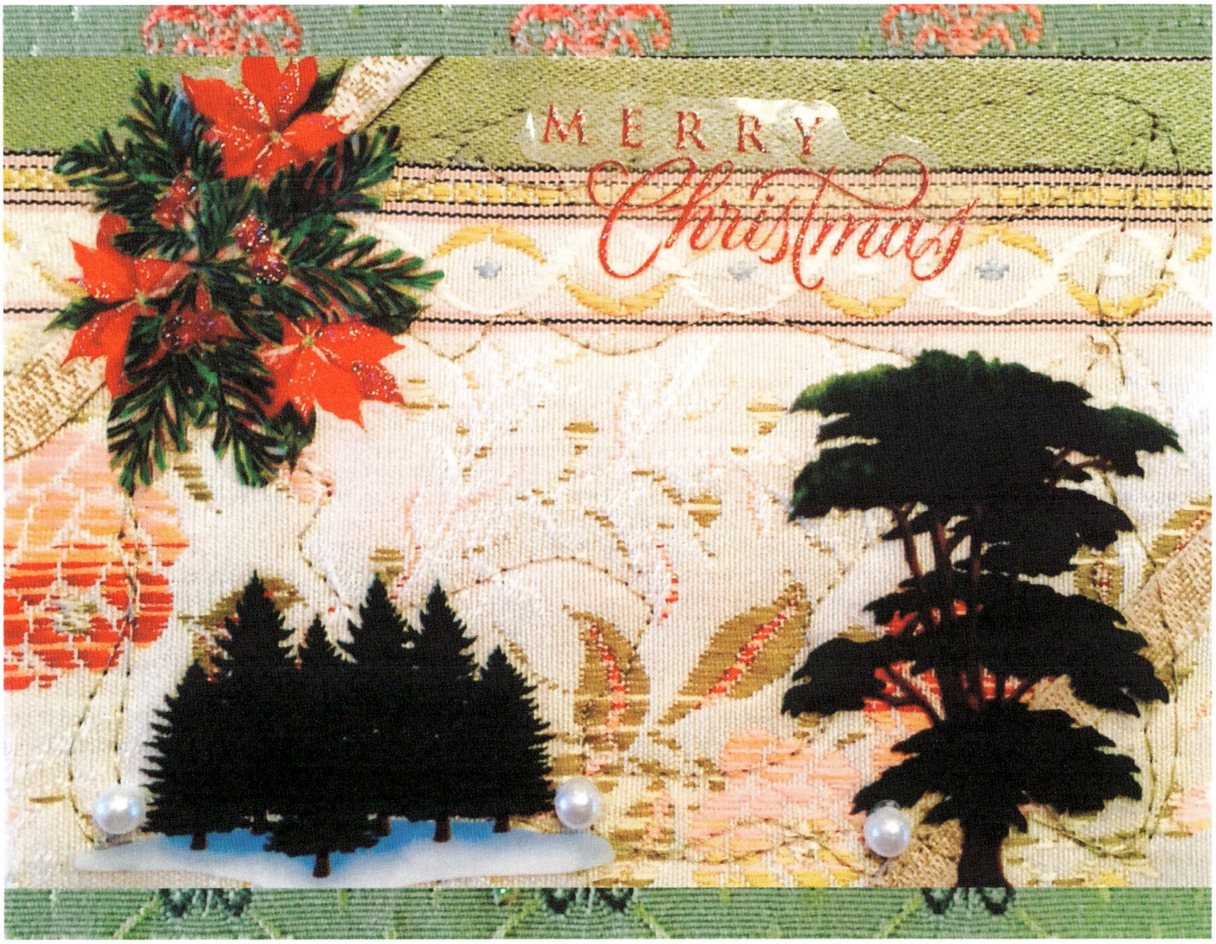
MERRY
Christmas

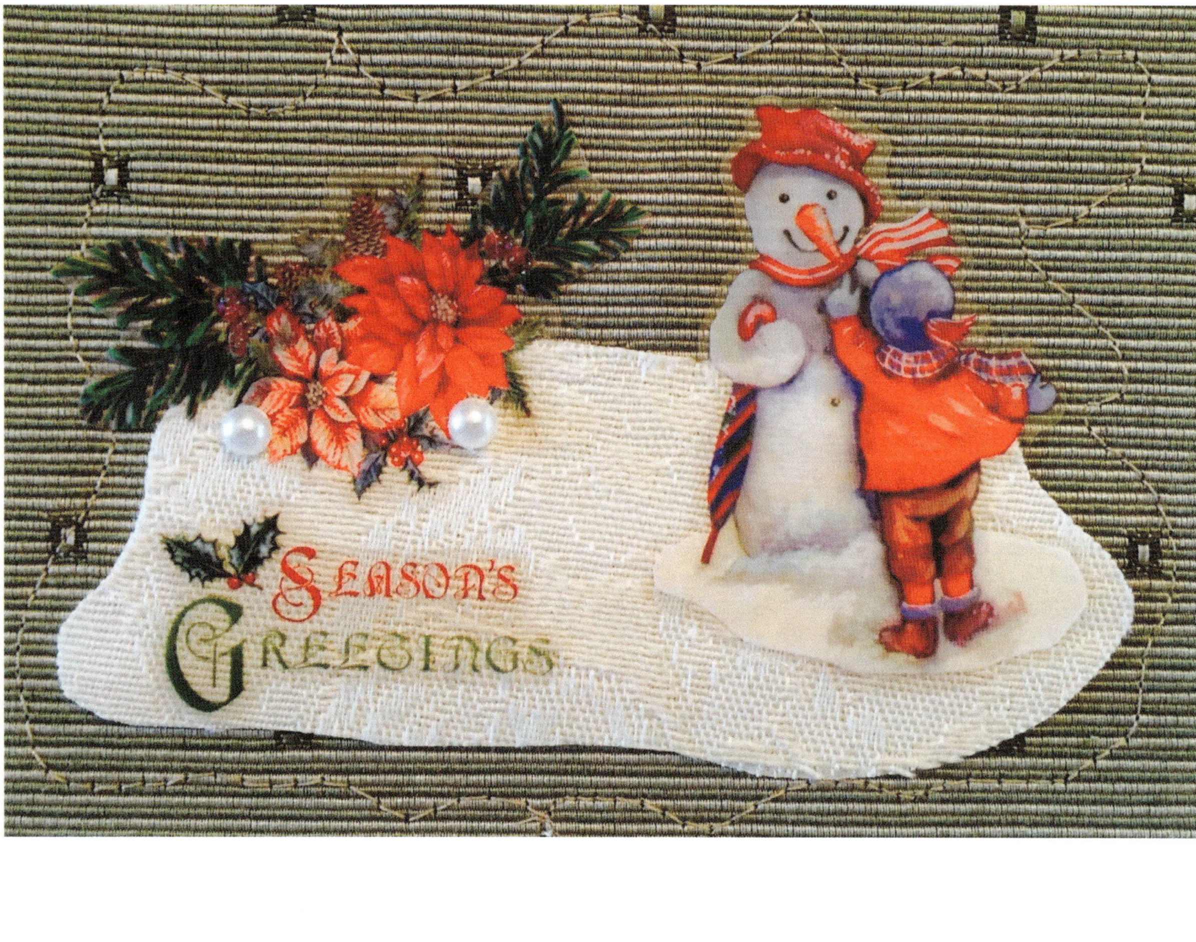
Season's
Greetings

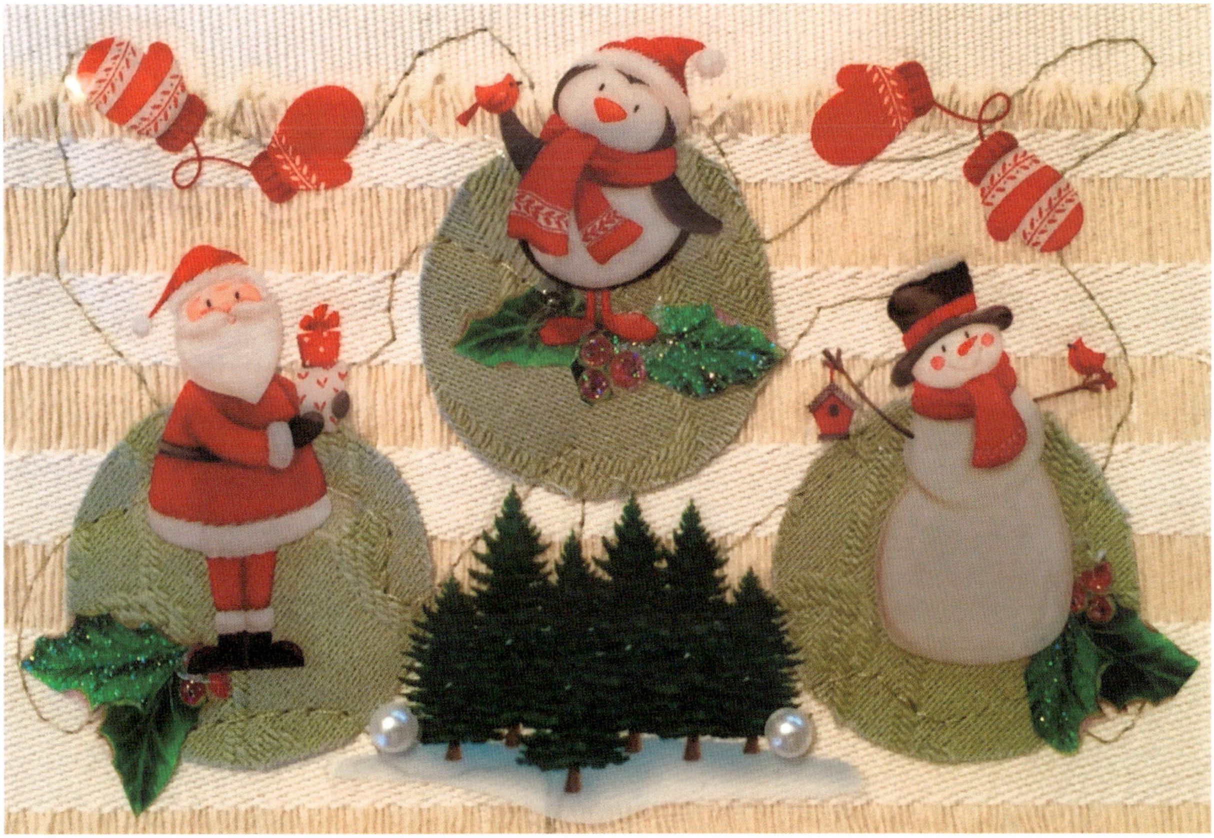

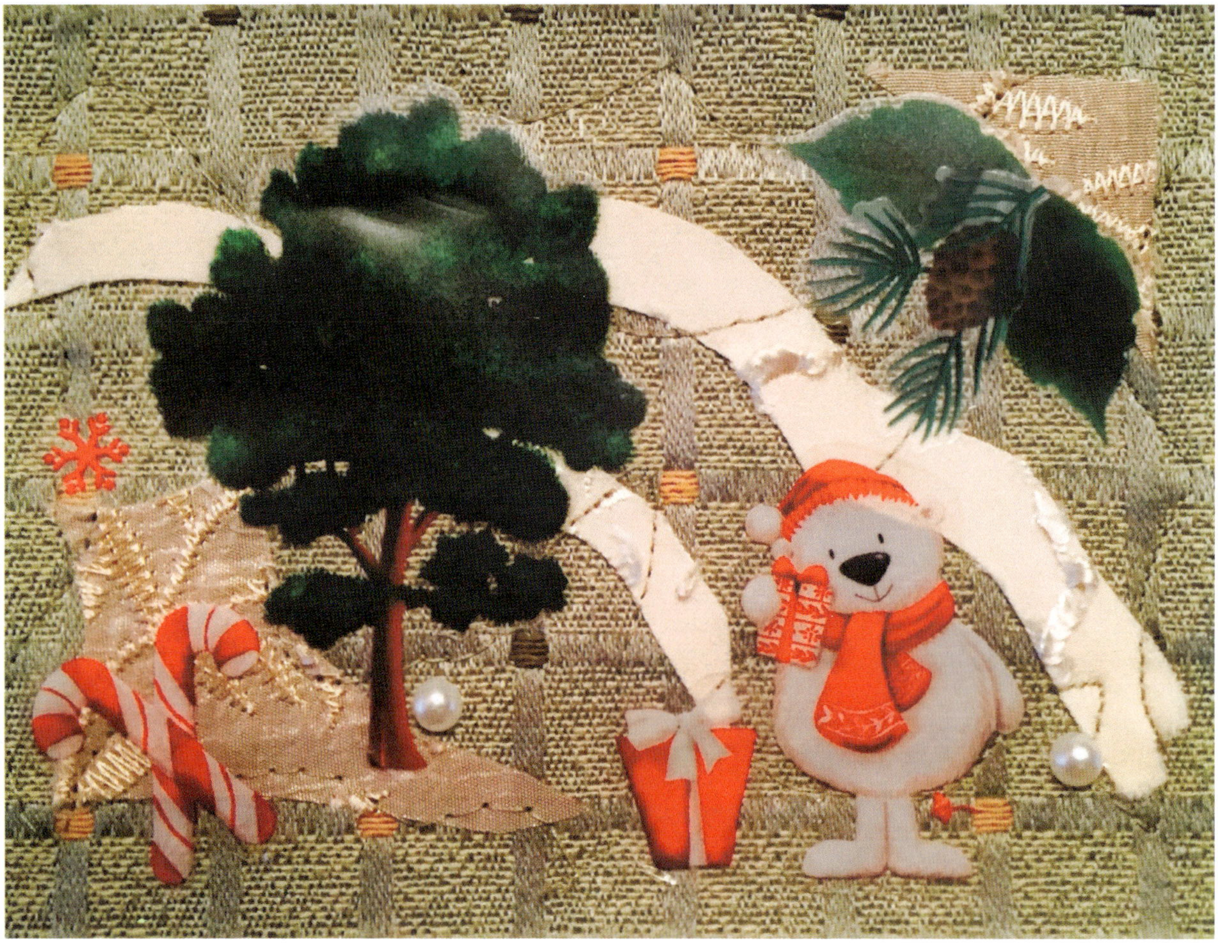

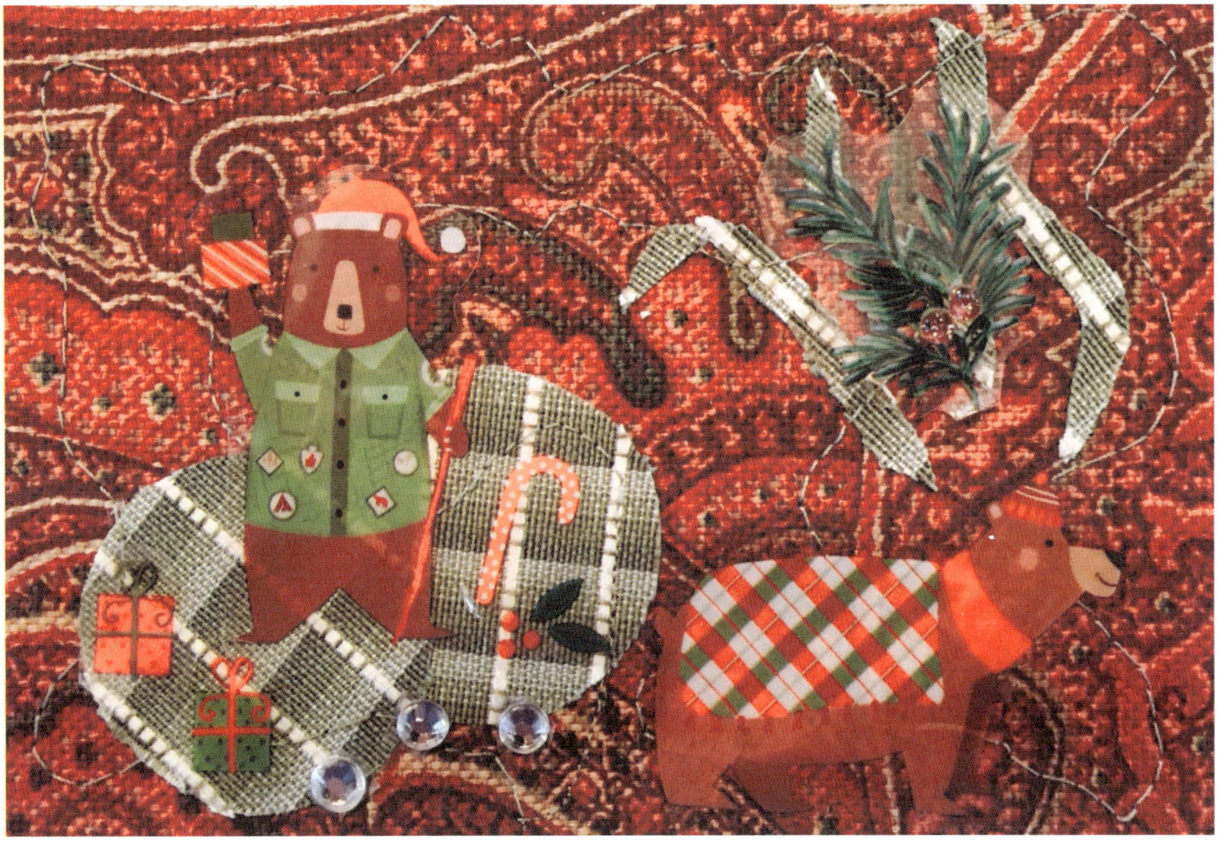

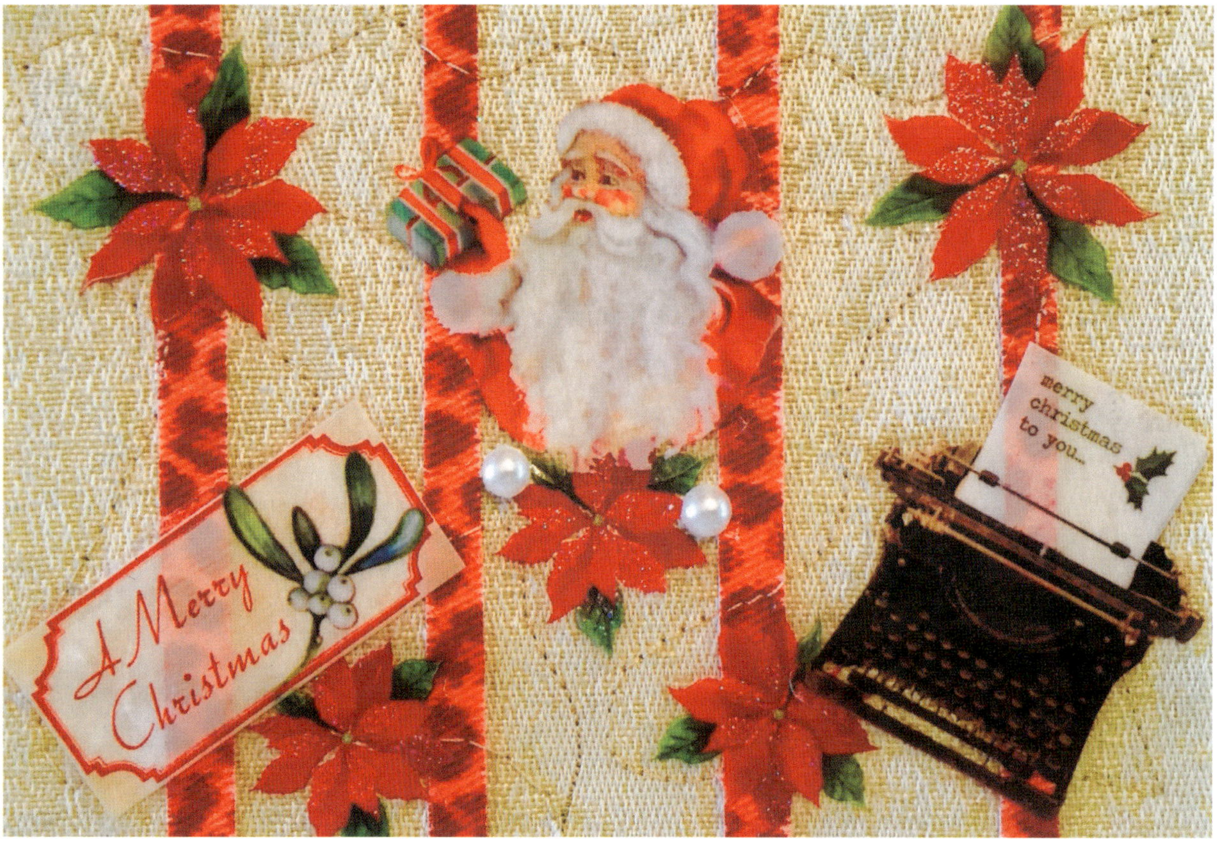
A Merry Christmas
merry christmas to you..

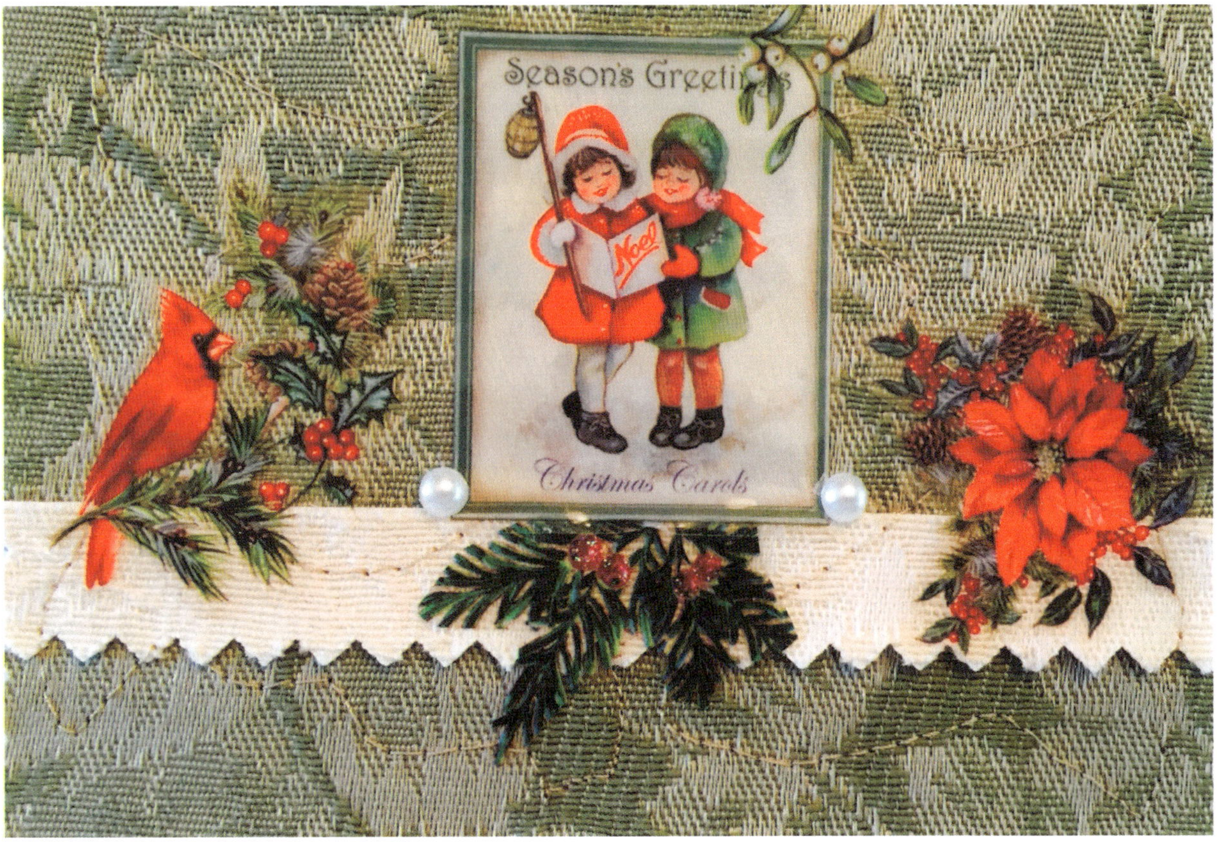
Season's Greetings
Noel
Christmas Carols

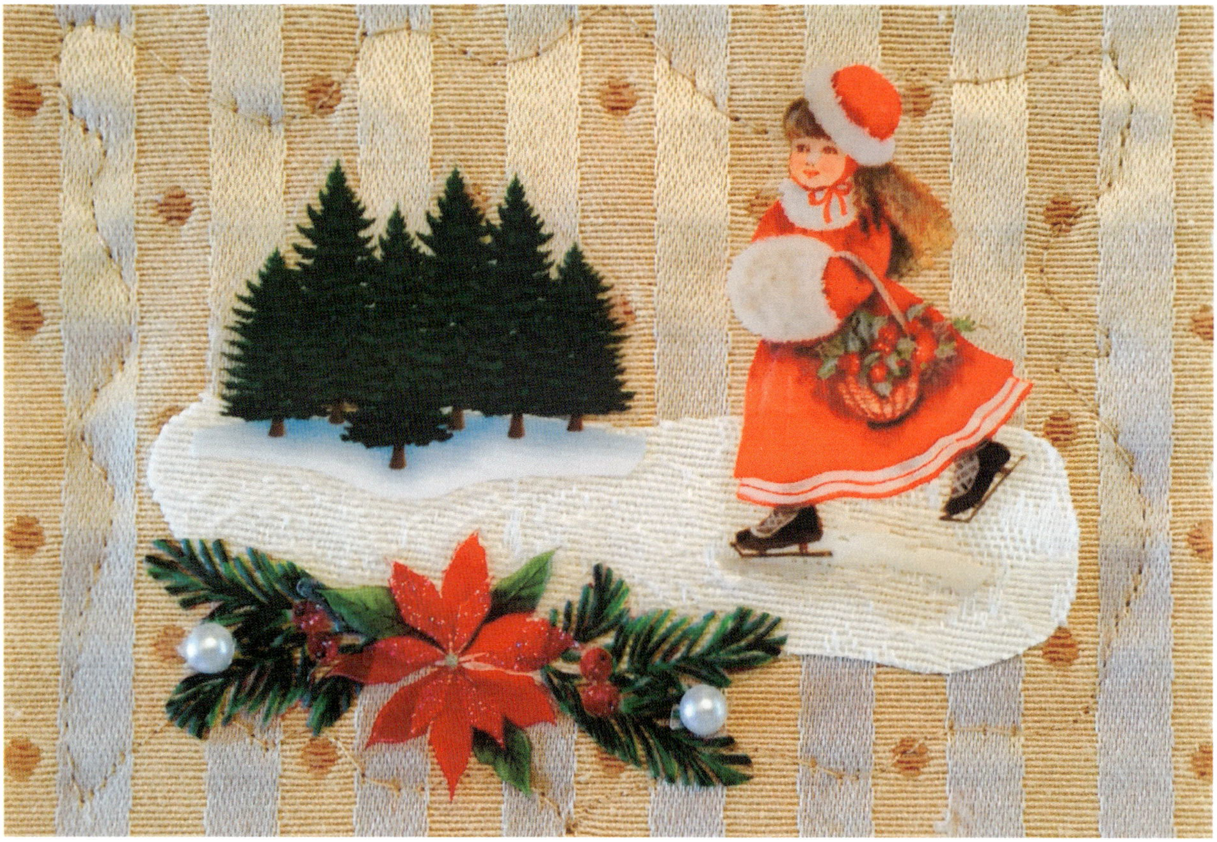

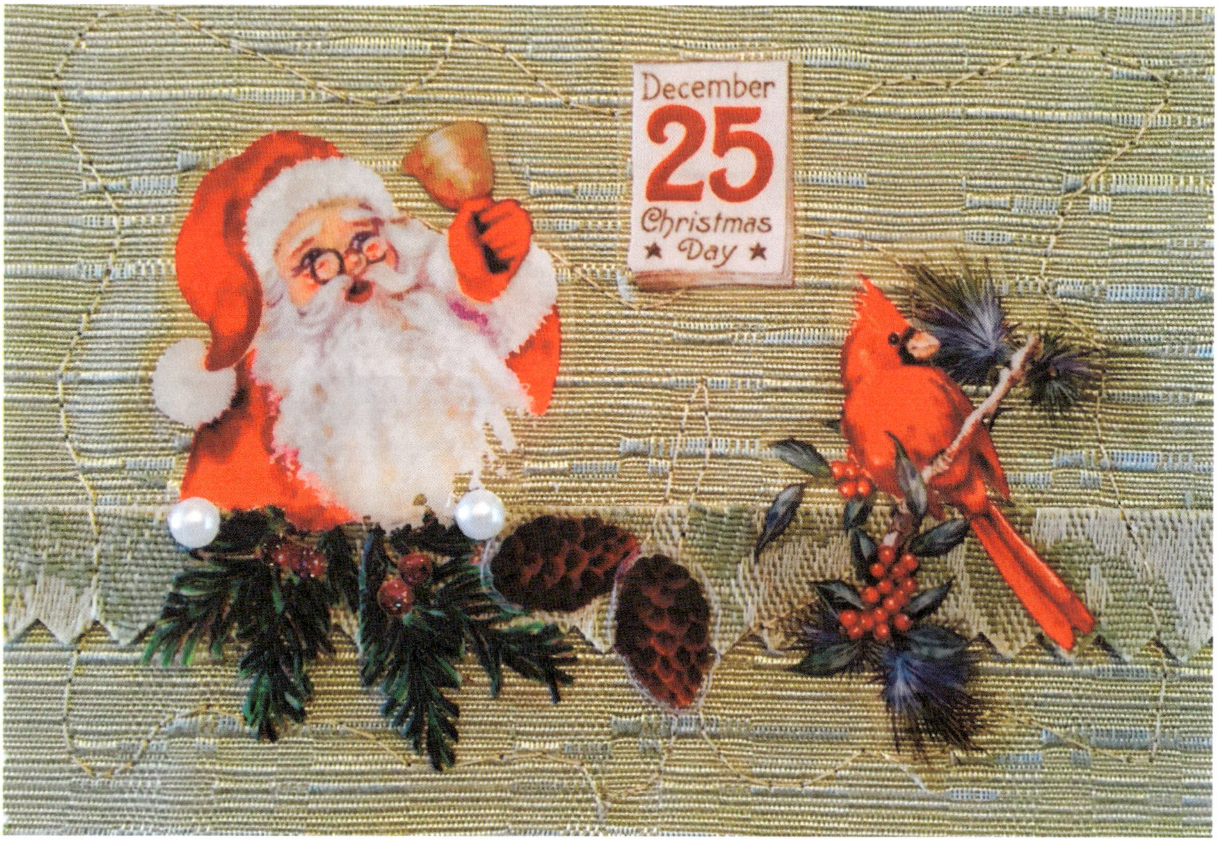
December
25
Christmas
Day

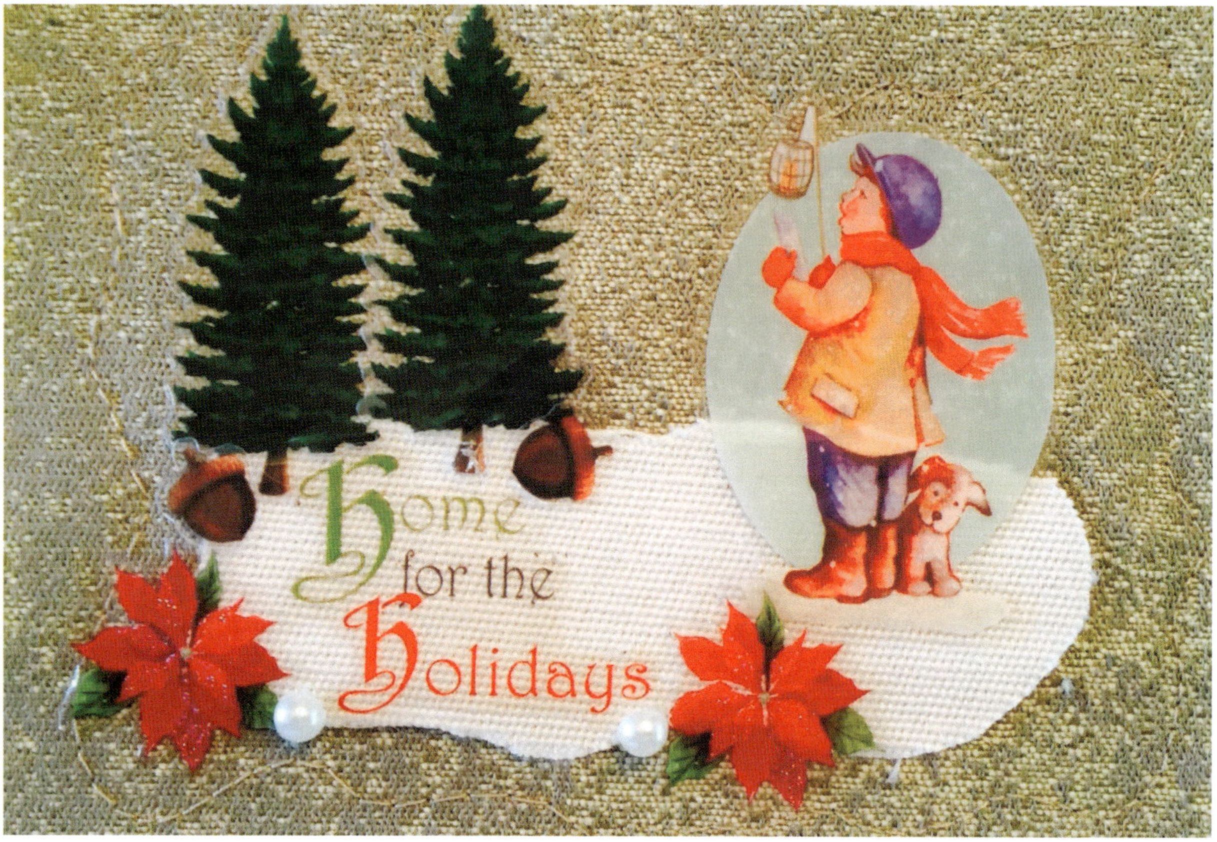
Home
for the
Holidays

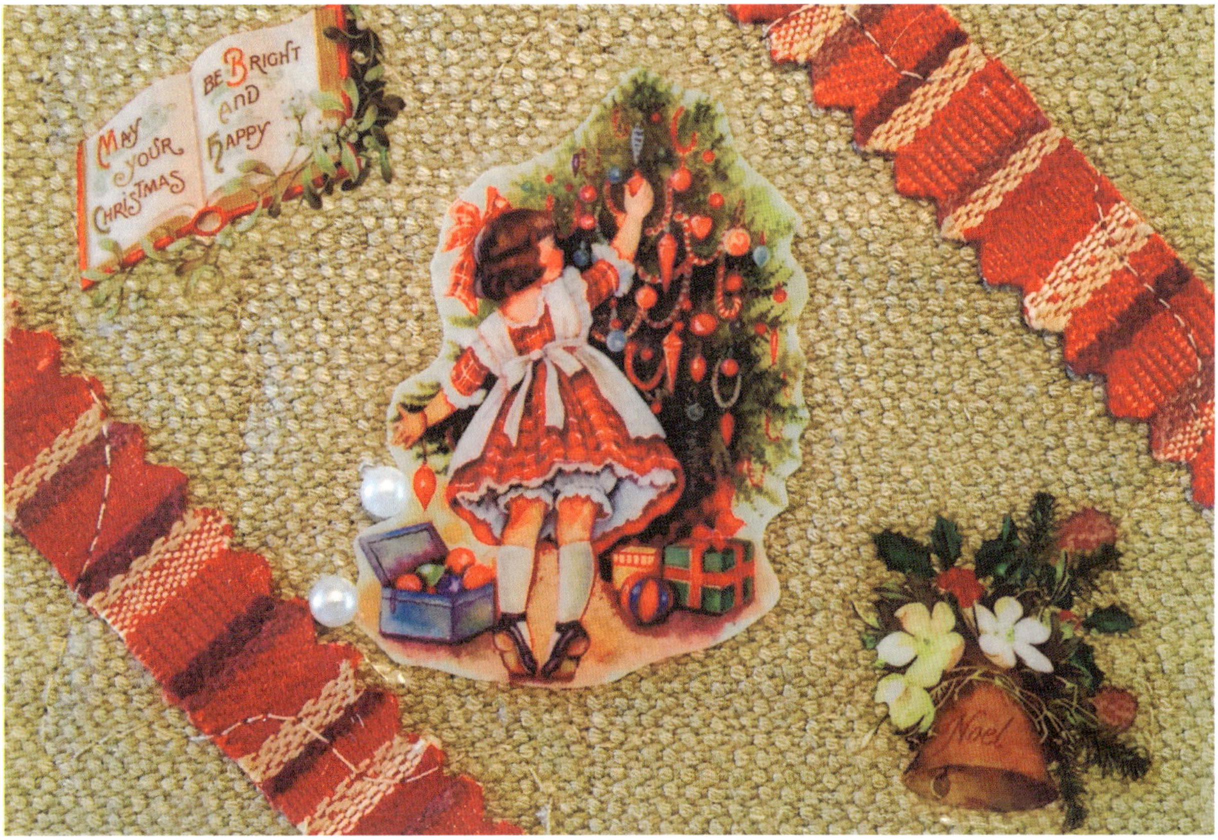
MAY YOUR CHRISTMAS
BE BRIGHT AND HAPPY
Noel

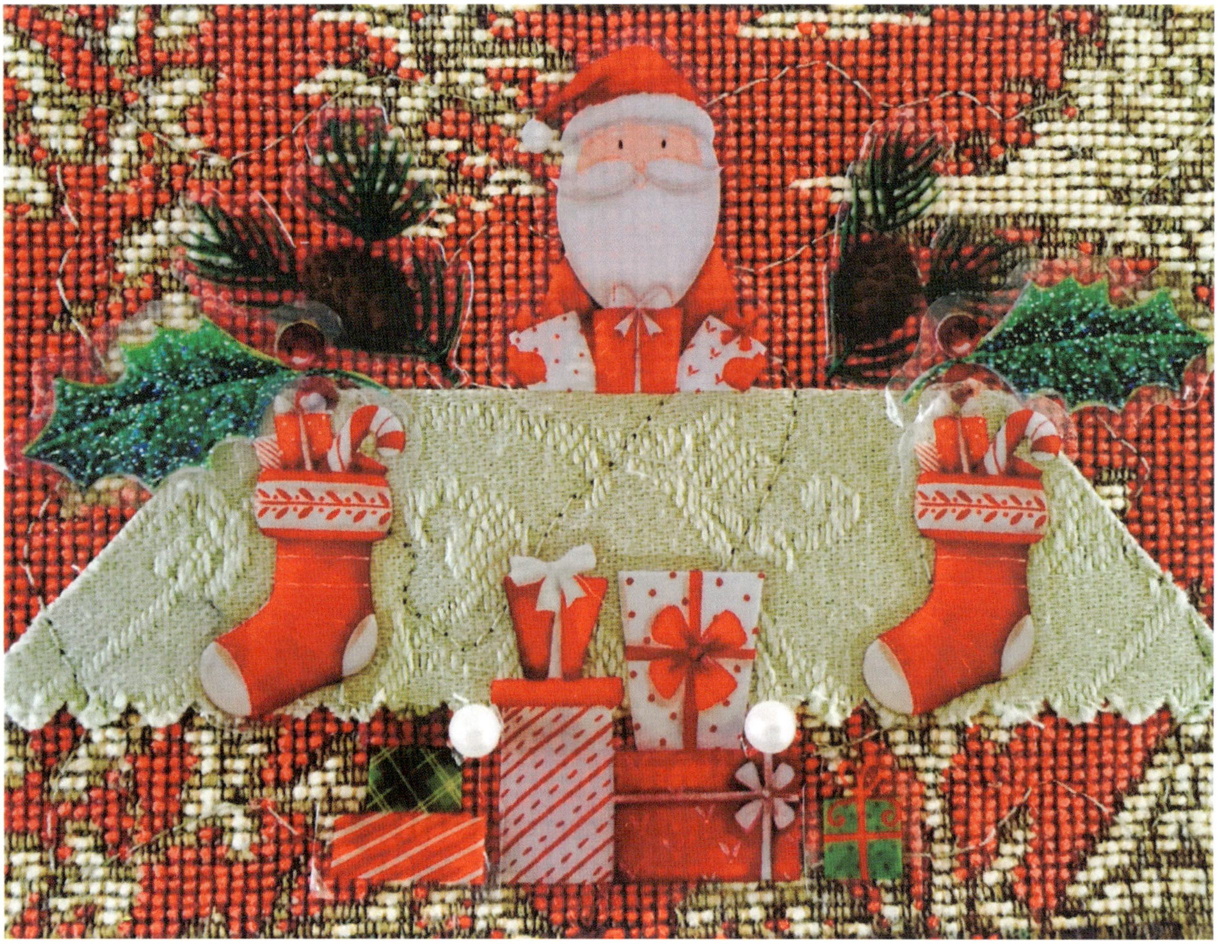

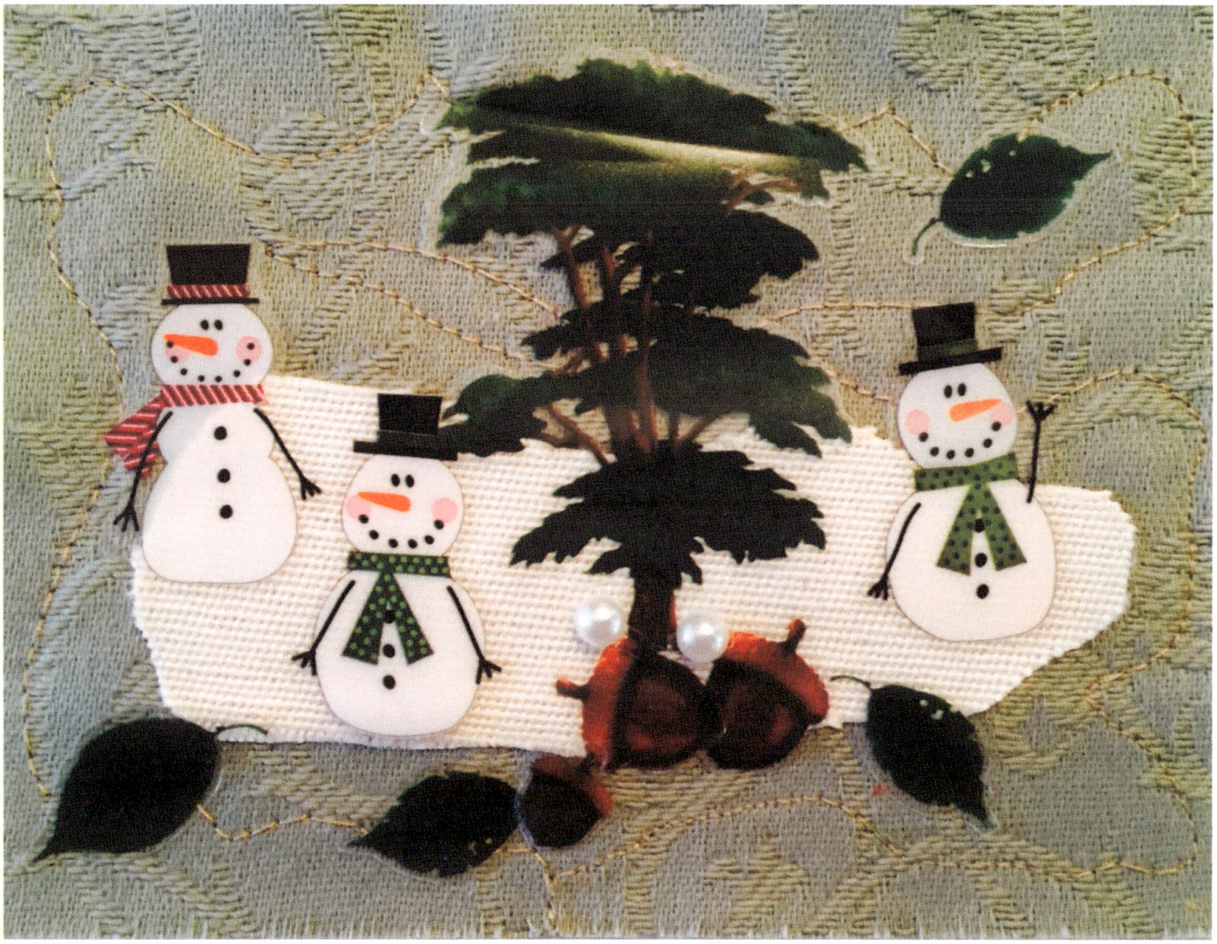

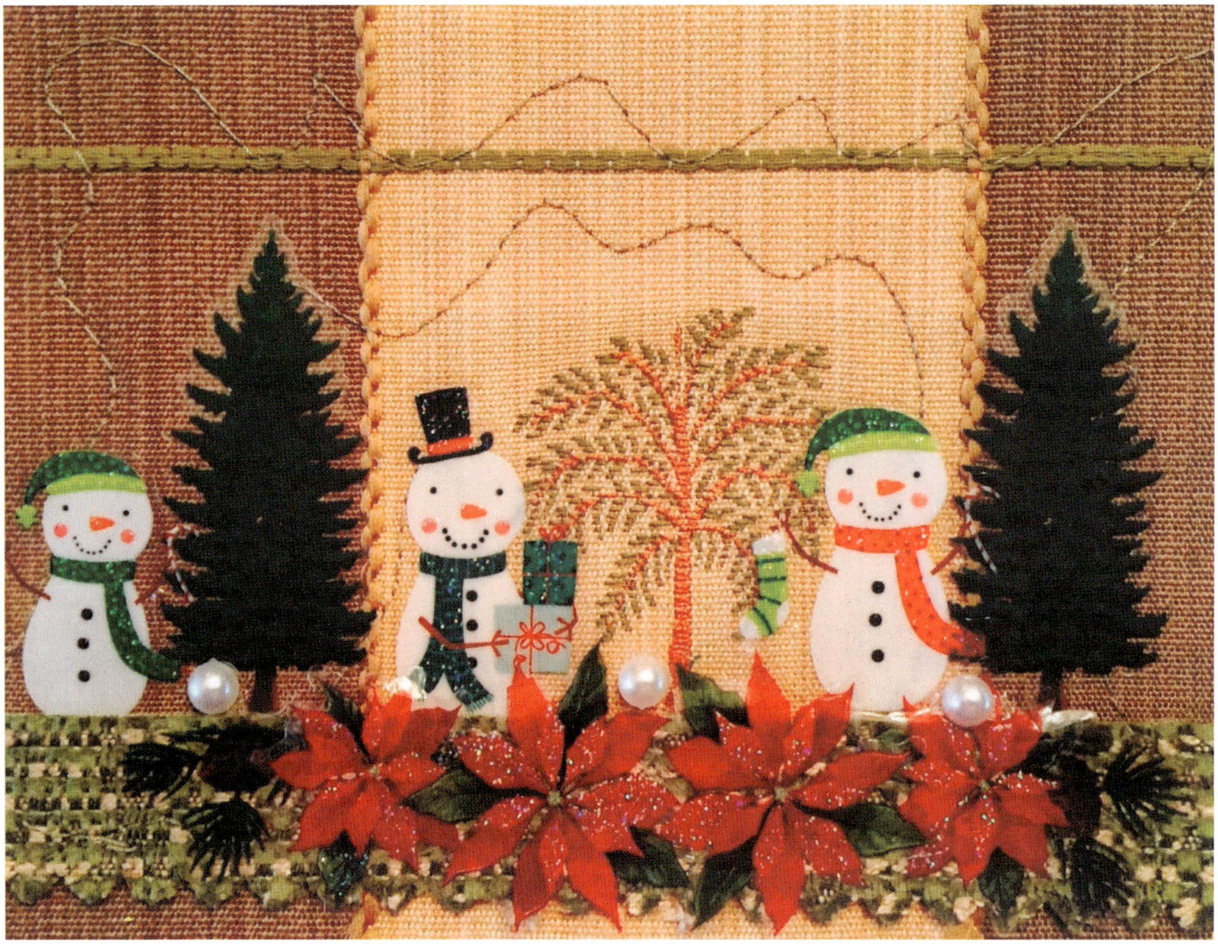

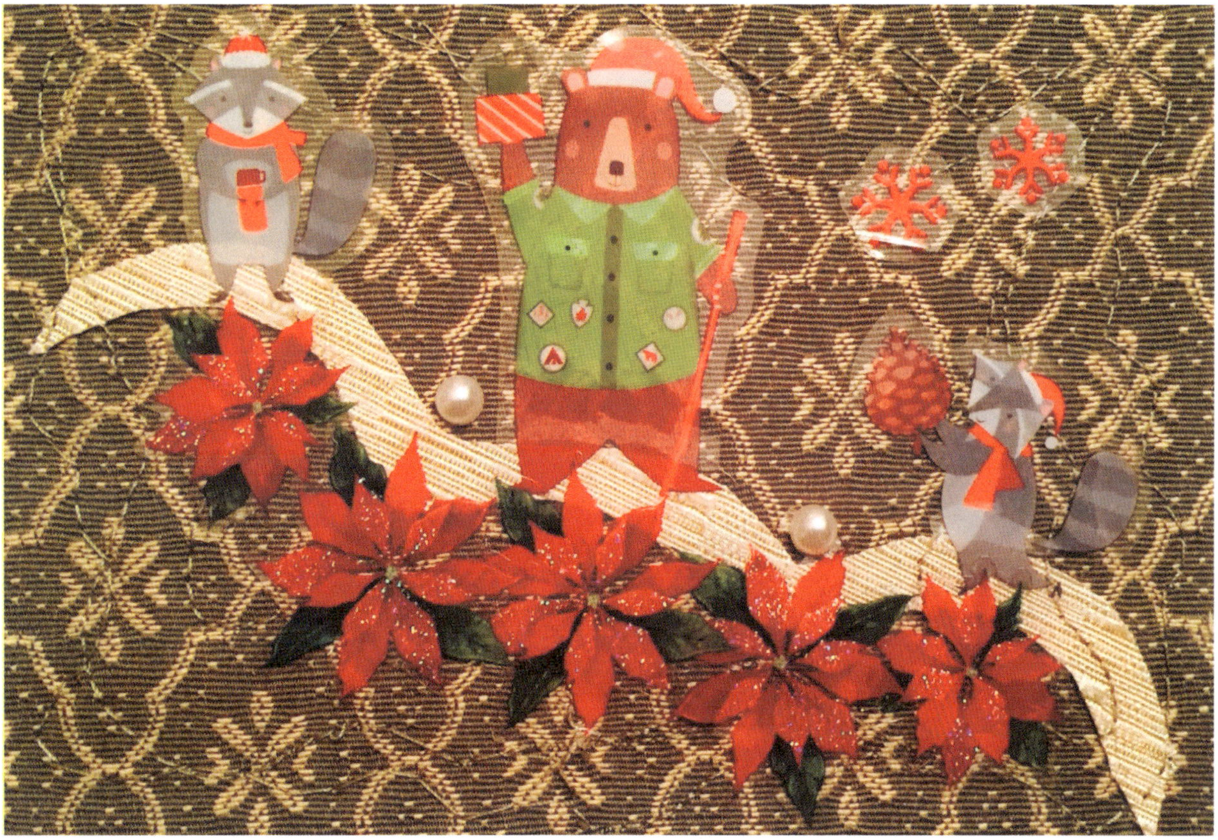

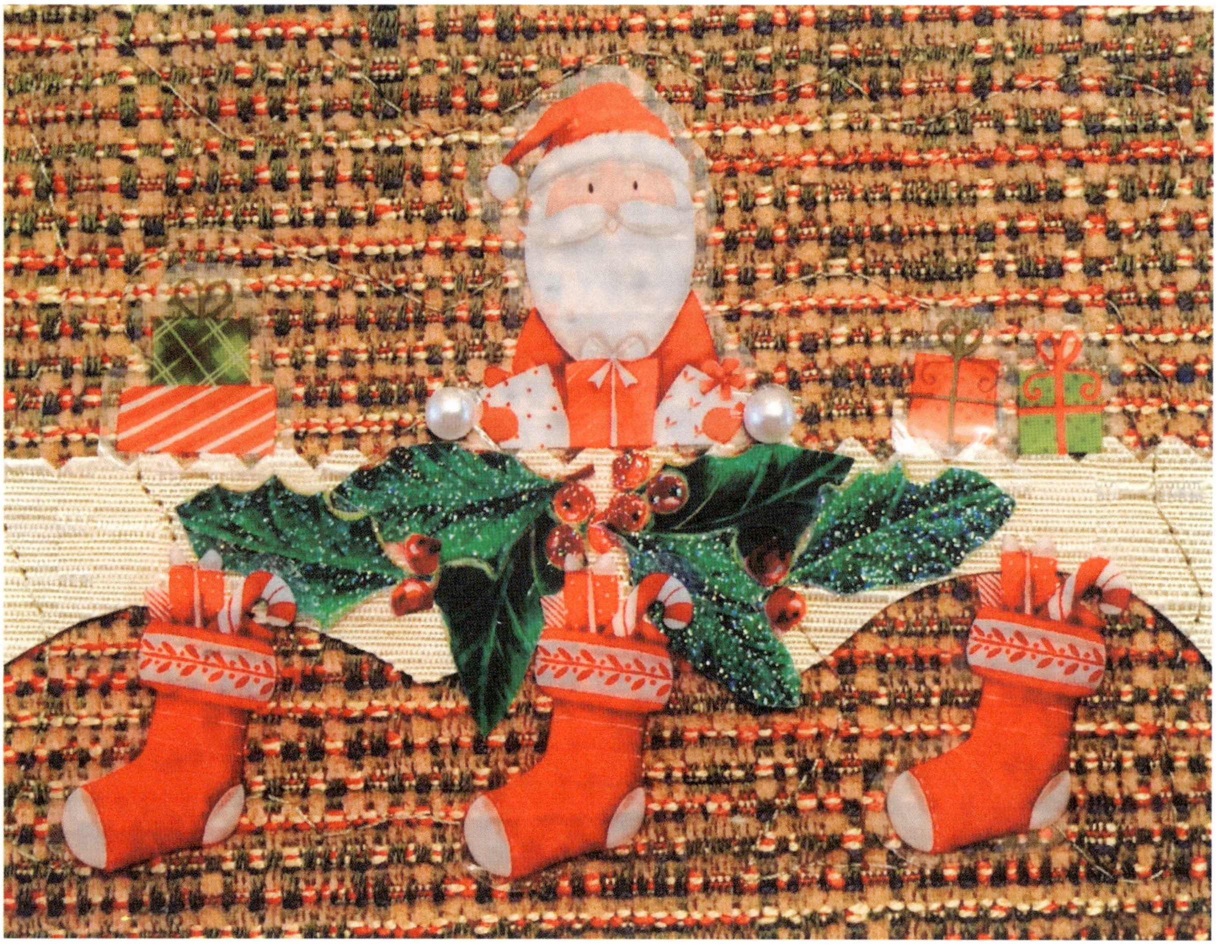

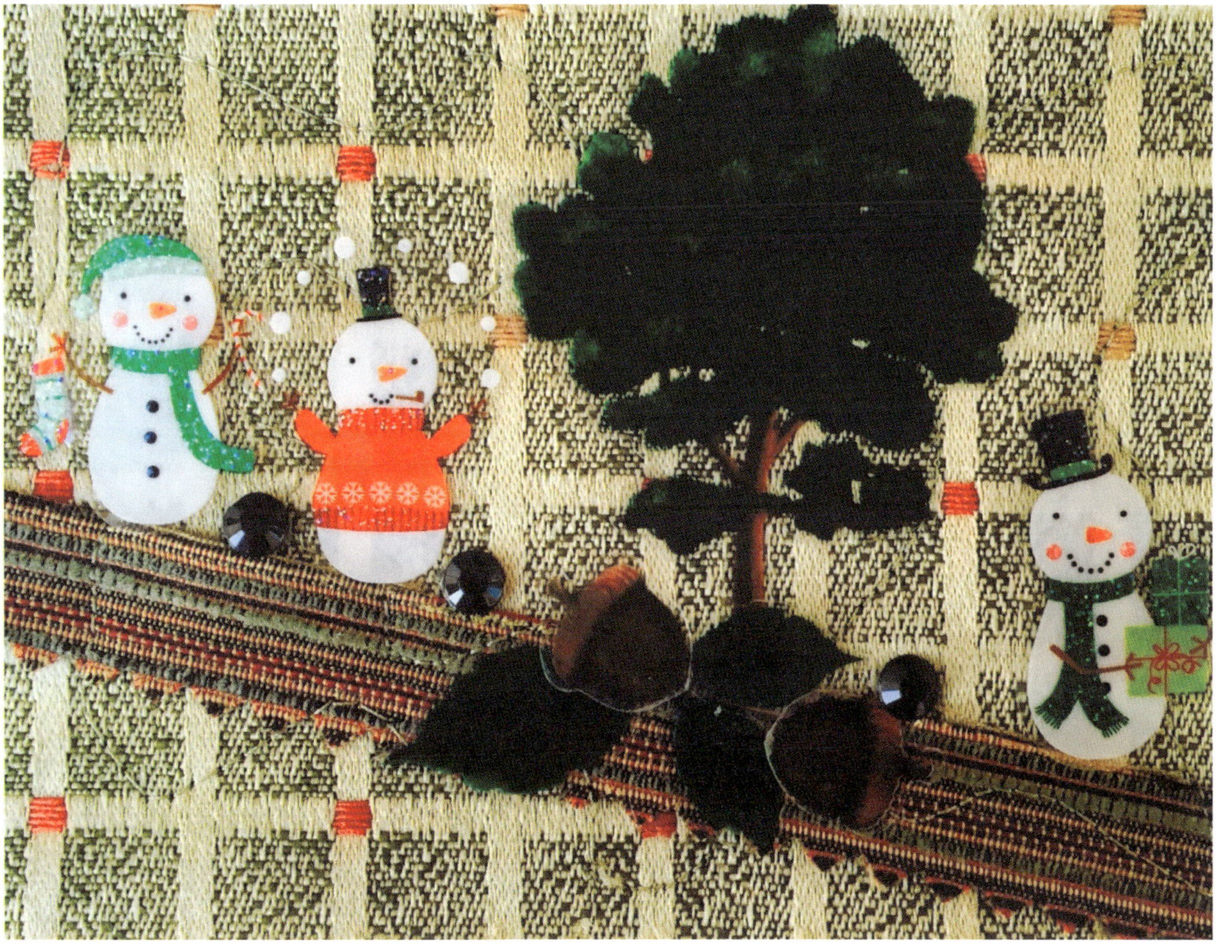

Afterword

These petite quilts have given people much pleasure. They look nice framed. A friend has sent them to older people in nursing homes and reports they bring tears to their eyes. In our busy world I hope these small quilts on a card give you ideas for quick and easy projects.

Acknowledgements

I owe gratitude to my son Robert Masten III who is my rock when it comes to computer skills. I would like to thank a fellow artist who I met briefly and gave me many sample upholstery books. These fabrics changed my cards dramatically.

Debby Masten Berard

About the Author

Debby Masten Berard is an experienced quilter with a degree from Appalachian State University. Highlights of her career include Embellished by Nature quilt pattern line, and a quilt that placed in a national competition. She resides in Southport, North Carolina and can be found online at Fineartamerica.com.

-Debby Berard

Printed in Dunstable, United Kingdom